AF598992

MACHINE LEARNING

GEORGE ANTHONY KULZ

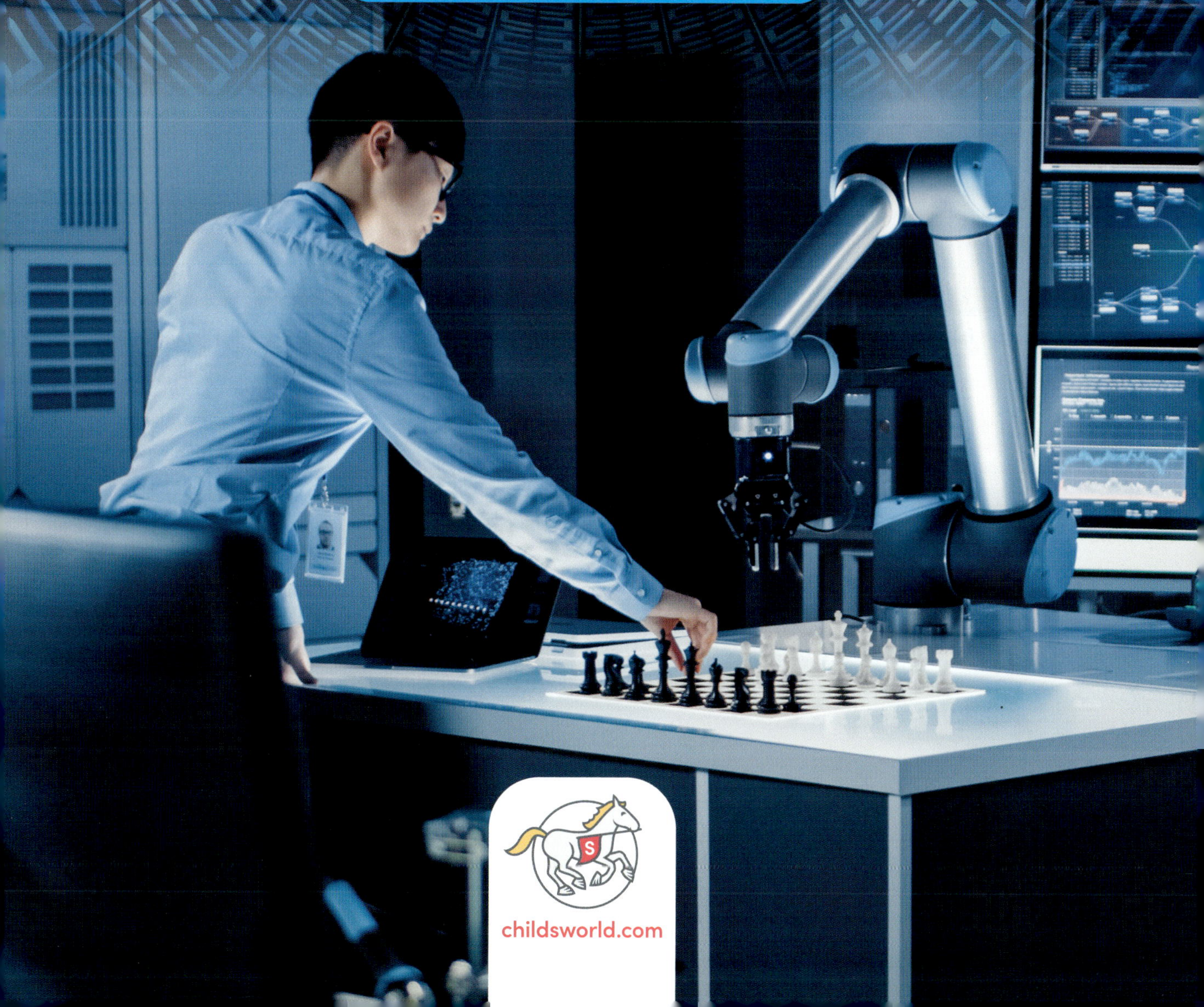

The Child's World
childsworld.com

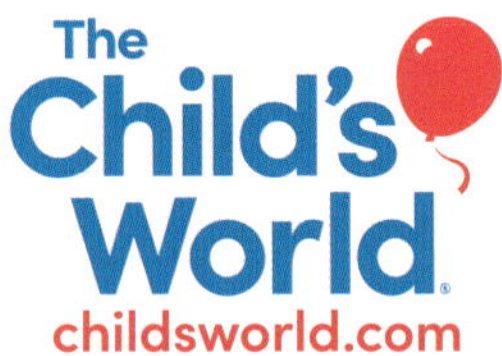

Published by The Child's World®
800-599-READ • www.childsworld.com

Photography Credits
Photographs ©: Shutterstock Images, cover, 1, 9, 10, 21; Roman Zaiets/Shutterstock Images, 5; Yakobchuk Viacheslav/Shutterstock Images, 6; Tommy Lee Walker/Shutterstock Images, 12; Pictures from History/Universal Images Group/Getty Images, 15; Lee Jin-man/AP Images, 17; Benvenuto Cellini/Shutterstock Images, 19 (wheel and car); Red Line Editorial, 19 (levels); Design elements from Tatiana Shepeleva/Shutterstock Images and Shutterstock Images

ISBN Information
9781503893825 (Reinforced Library Binding)
9781503894648 (Portable Document Format)
9781503895461 (Online Multi-user eBook)
9781503896284 (Electronic Publication)

LCCN 2024942883

Printed in the United States of America

BRINGING THE WORLD TO YOUNG READERS 1968

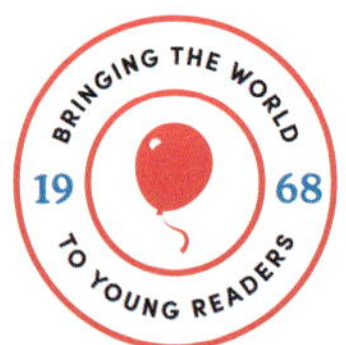

ABOUT THE AUTHOR

George Anthony Kulz holds a master's degree in computer engineering. He is a member of the Society of Children's Book Writers and Illustrators. He writes for children and adults.

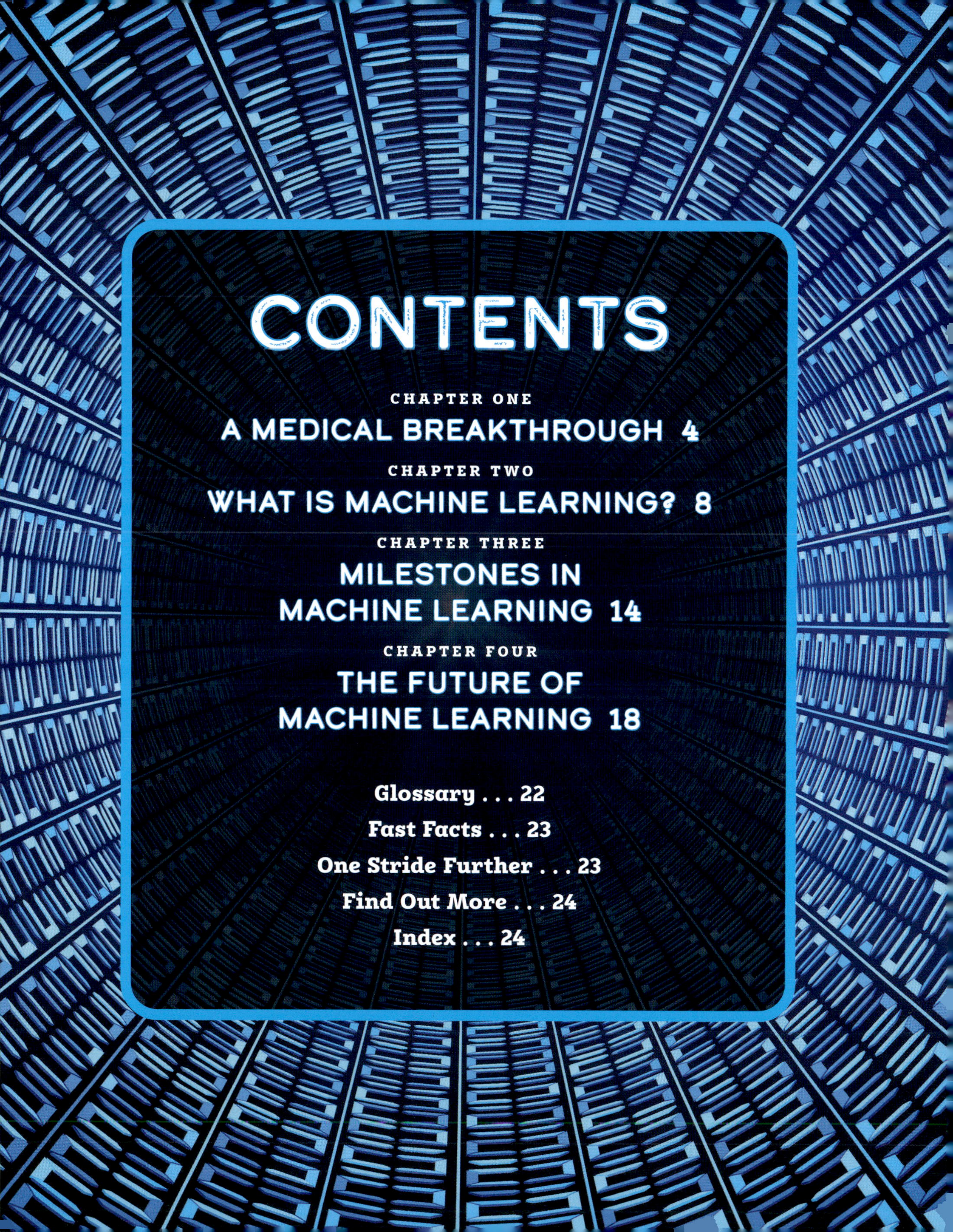

CONTENTS

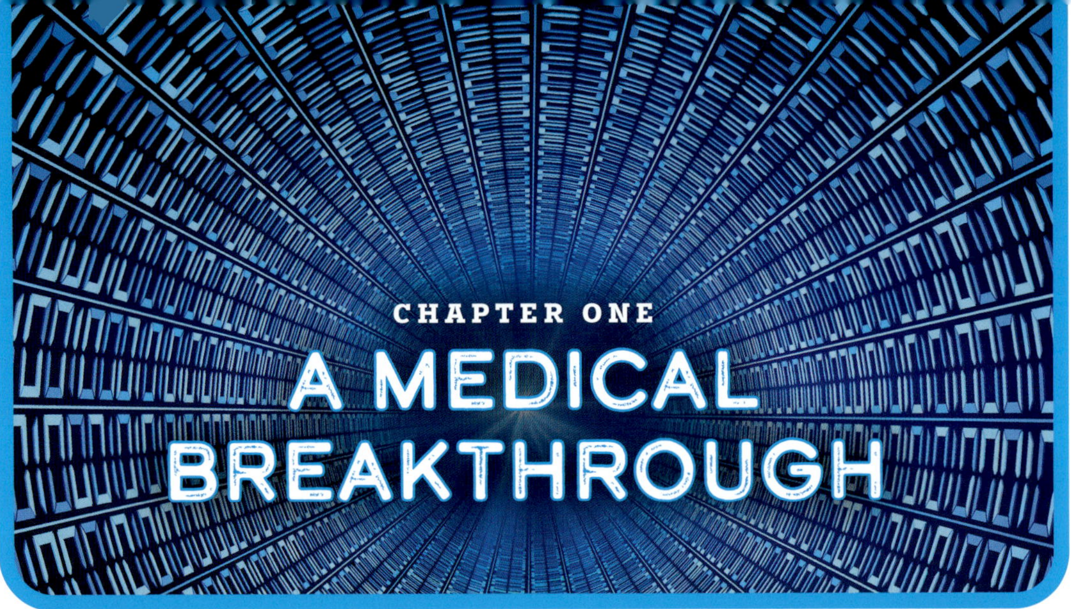

CHAPTER ONE

A MEDICAL BREAKTHROUGH

A man places a cap on his head. The cap is covered in **sensors**. He is taking part in an experiment. A researcher asks him to think a few specific sentences. "Good afternoon! I hope you're doing well. I'll start with a cappuccino, please, with an extra shot of espresso."

The man repeats the sentences in his head. A computer nearby then displays some text. "Afternoon! You well? Cappuccino, Xtra shot. Espresso."

The test was a success. The computer showed what the man was thinking. It had essentially read his mind! Researchers did the same experiment with other test subjects. The computer was able to correctly display their thoughts 40 percent of the time.

Doctors use caps with sensors on them for lots of reasons. The caps can help doctors understand disorders in a patient's brain.

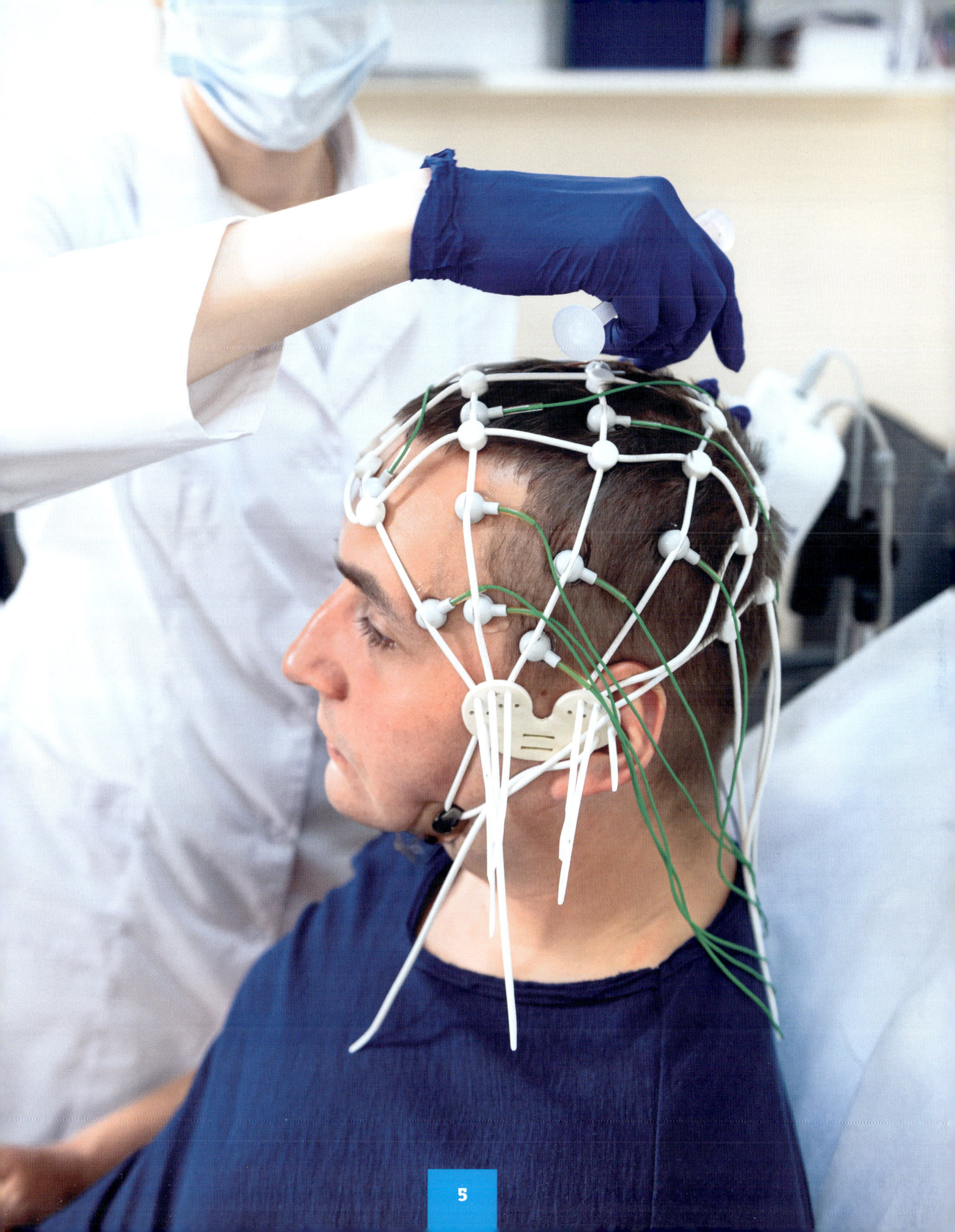

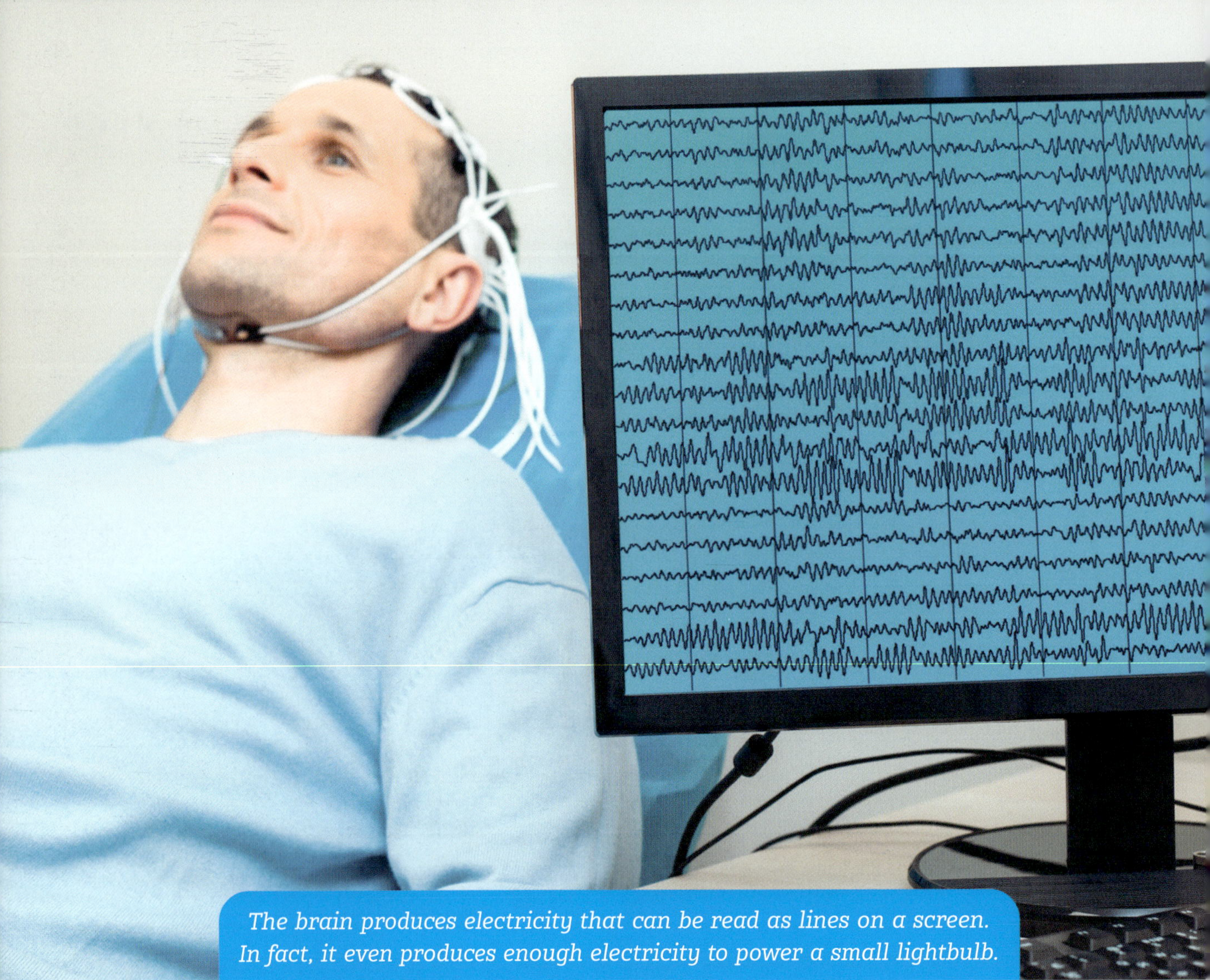

The brain produces electricity that can be read as lines on a screen. In fact, it even produces enough electricity to power a small lightbulb.

Researchers from a university in Sydney, Australia, developed this technology. They called their invention DeWave. It works by measuring electrical activity in the brain. When someone thinks about something, brain cells create electrical **impulses**. These impulses travel among brain cells.

With DeWave, a machine records these impulses as wavy lines. The wavy lines are turned into words using machine learning (ML). Machine learning is a field of computer science. It focuses on making computers mimic the way that people learn. ML allows DeWave to turn the wavy lines into words that resemble what the person thought.

Devices like DeWave are giving people hope. Many people have trouble speaking or moving. This could be due to a medical condition or other reasons. Someday they may be able to speak or move using devices powered by ML. This technology has the potential to enrich people's lives.

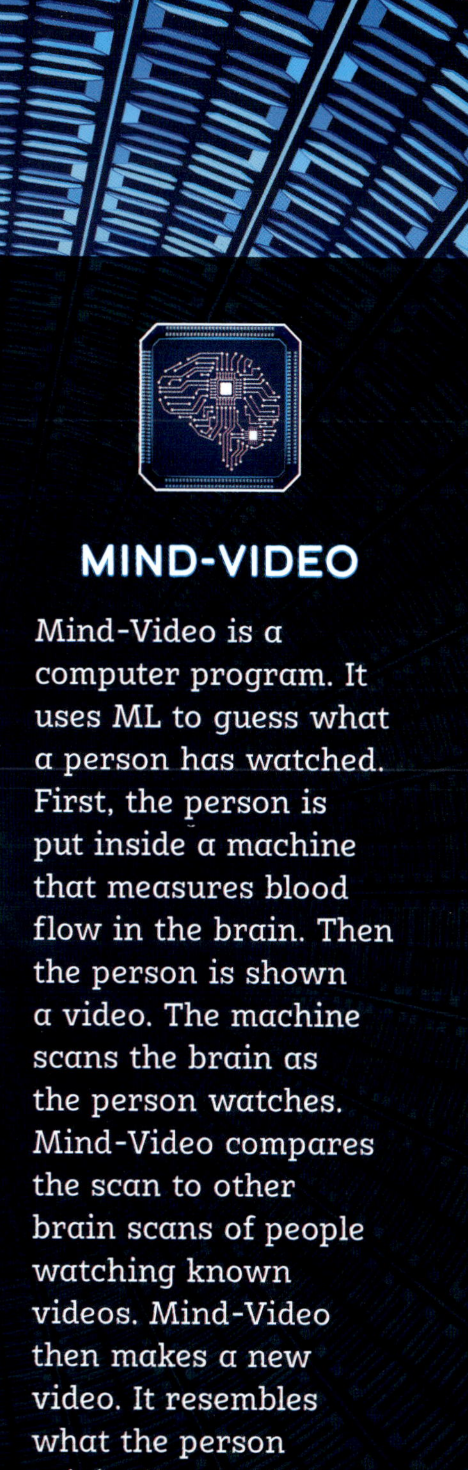

MIND-VIDEO

Mind-Video is a computer program. It uses ML to guess what a person has watched. First, the person is put inside a machine that measures blood flow in the brain. Then the person is shown a video. The machine scans the brain as the person watches. Mind-Video compares the scan to other brain scans of people watching known videos. Mind-Video then makes a new video. It resembles what the person originally watched.

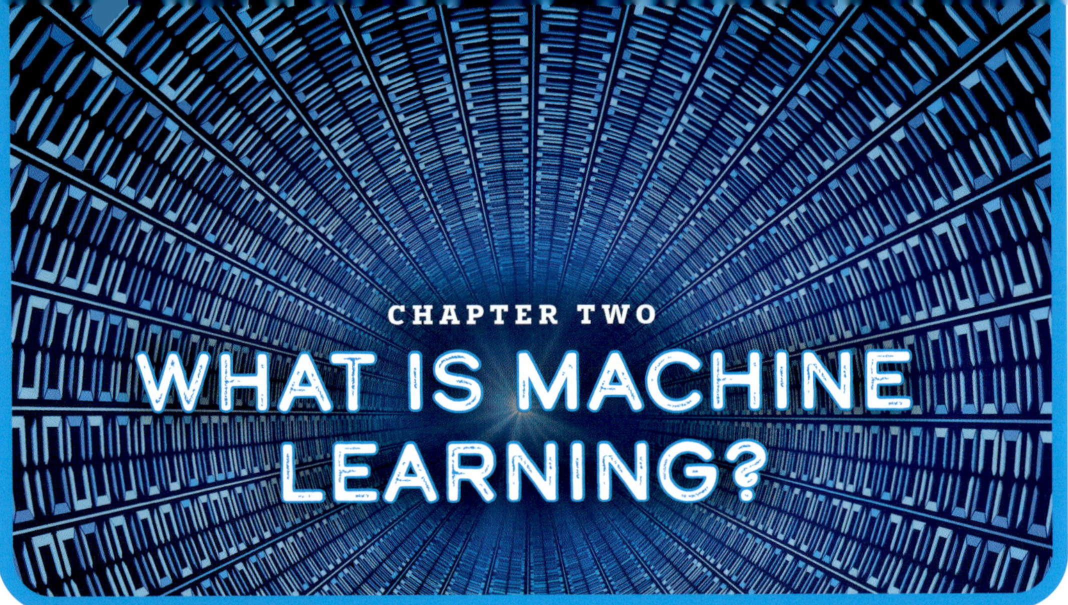

CHAPTER TWO

WHAT IS MACHINE LEARNING?

Machine learning is a field of artificial intelligence (AI). AI is the ability of computers to do things humans normally do. In order to learn, a computer needs instructions. It also needs a large amount of **data**.

All computers need to be told what to do. Step-by-step instructions are given to them so that they can solve problems. These instructions are called algorithms. An algorithm is like a recipe for making a cake. The recipe has all the necessary steps needed for the cake to come out perfectly.

People give computers instructions by writing algorithms in coding languages, which computers can understand.

Data labeling is also called data annotation. The word annotation *means the act of adding notes to something.*

ML algorithms tell computers how to learn things from the data given to them. There are four main types of these algorithms. The differences between the types have to do with how the data is labeled. Labeling allows ML algorithms to make sense of data. For example, an ML algorithm might be given data consisting of photographs. One way to label the data is by noting which photographs contain people. Another label could note which photographs contain animals. Labeling allows people to tell the computer what to focus on in the data.

The first type of algorithm is called supervised learning. It involves teaching the computer using labeled data. If the computer does not understand the data, a user has to help train the computer. The second type is called semi-supervised learning. Here, some labeled data and some unlabeled data are given to the computer. The computer learns information about the data. It then uses that data to try labeling the unlabeled data. Unsupervised learning is the third type of algorithm. The computer tries to find patterns in unlabeled data with no help from humans.

Large collections of data are often stored on computers called servers.

Reinforcement learning is the fourth type of ML algorithm. In reinforcement learning, people give the algorithm feedback as it makes decisions. Over time, the computer learns to make the right decisions. It uses what it learns on any future data.

For example, reinforcement learning algorithms can be taught how to play chess.

A large amount of data is needed for any ML algorithm. Otherwise, the algorithm might not learn enough about the data. This could cause it to make mistakes when given new data. For example, an ML algorithm might be designed to tell whether an image contains a car. If the algorithm is only trained on images of trucks, it might not spot smaller cars. The algorithm might also make mistakes if the data is labeled improperly. For example, certain images might contain cars that were not labeled. This could confuse the algorithm.

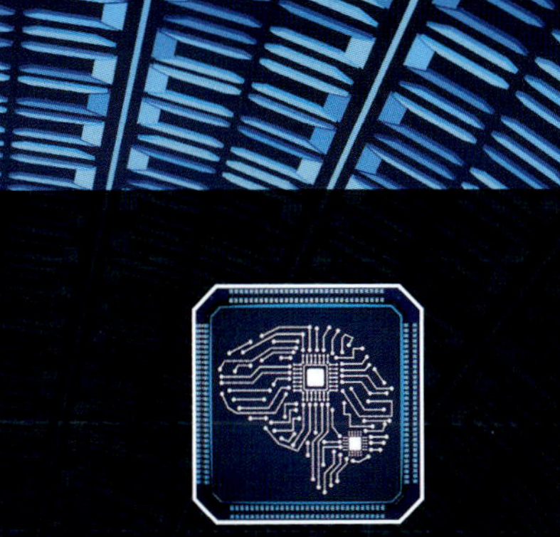

DEEP LEARNING

Deep learning is a type of machine learning. A deep learning algorithm finds patterns in large amounts of data. The algorithm uses neural networks to find these patterns. A neural network is a program made up of many smaller programs that work like human brain cells. Each part receives data, **processes** that data, and produces a result. Working together, the parts of a neural network can solve challenging problems.

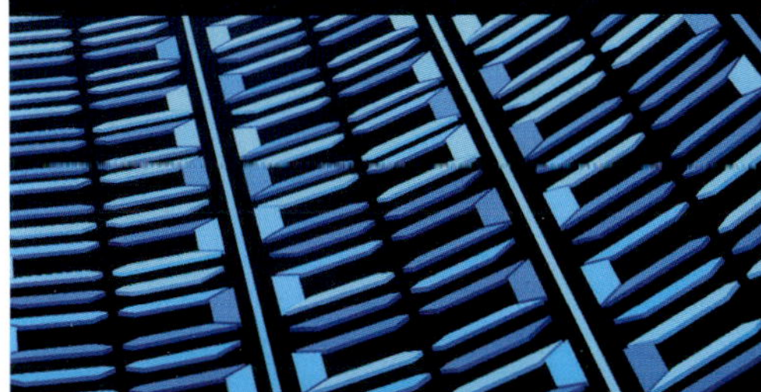

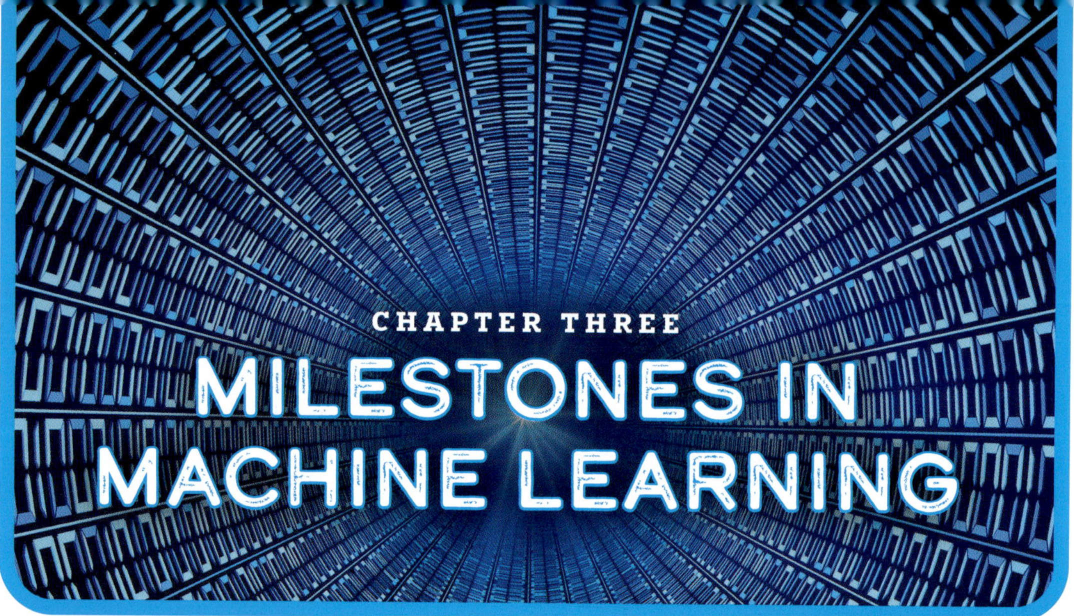

CHAPTER THREE

MILESTONES IN MACHINE LEARNING

Machine learning had its beginnings in the 1940s. British mathematician Alan Turing came up with the idea of the modern computer. He thought computers could be used to solve a wide range of problems. Turing was also one of the first people to think about AI. He predicted that computers would be able to learn from experience.

In 1951, Evelyn Fix and Joseph Hodges came up with the idea of the k-nearest neighbors algorithm. This algorithm **classifies** data points into provided groups. When a new point is given to the algorithm, the algorithm checks what group the points closest to the new point belong to. The programmer chooses how many points the algorithm checks.

Alan Turing was born on June 23, 1912. He used his mathematical skills to help Britain during World War II (1939–1945).

These points are called neighbors of the new point. The algorithm then puts the new point into the group containing the largest number of its neighbors. The k-nearest neighbors algorithm is a simple kind of machine learning. It is used to classify data in many different fields. These include finance and health care.

Arthur Samuel created one of the first machine learning programs in the 1950s. He wrote a program that learned to play the game checkers. Games are a good way to train machine learning algorithms. Games make it easy for the algorithms to measure their progress. Winning the game gives the algorithm a clear goal. Samuel's program used reinforcement learning as it played thousands of games of checkers against itself. Over time, it improved. Eventually, it was good enough to beat a human player.

Another game algorithm, AlphaGo, was created by the company DeepMind in 2014. AlphaGo used ML to learn how to play the board game Go. This game is far more complex than checkers. AlphaGo was given large amounts of information on past Go games. It then used reinforcement learning by playing games against itself. In 2016, it defeated the world's top human Go player.

During AlphaGo's match against the world's top human Go player (right), a computer scientist who worked on AlphaGo placed game pieces on the board based on the computer's instructions.

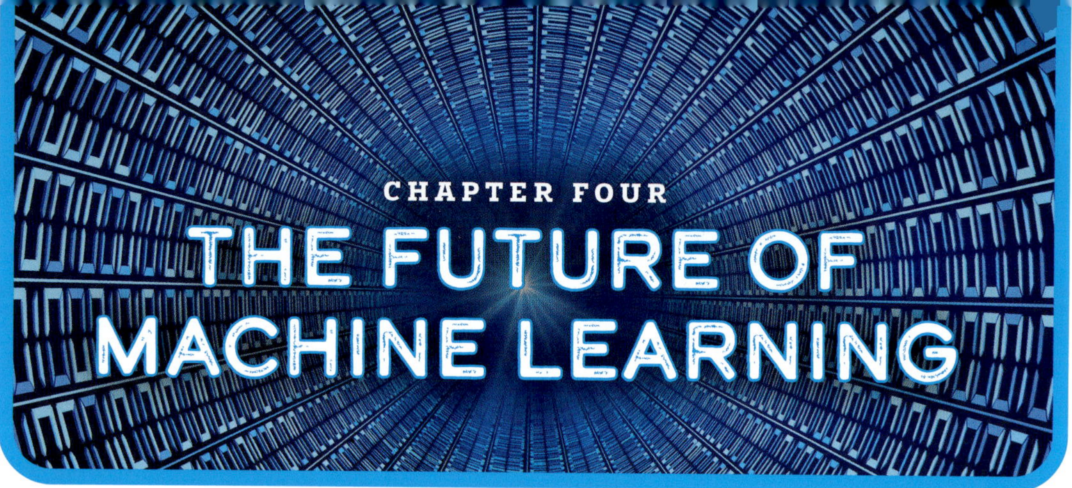

CHAPTER FOUR

THE FUTURE OF MACHINE LEARNING

Experts expect machine learning to be used in many new ways in the future. One of the biggest advances in ML is computer vision. This technology helps computers recognize objects in images. People train computer vision algorithms by giving them lots of images. When a computer receives a new image, it processes the image based on its training data.

One important application of computer vision is in driver assistance technology. Vehicles with this technology use computers to help people drive. Some vehicles can speed up or slow down on their own. Others can control the steering wheel. Computer vision helps these vehicles make the right driving decisions. In 2023, there were more than 30 million vehicles on the road using driver assistance technology. In the future, vehicles may be fully **autonomous**. This will require advances in computer vision and machine learning.

SIX LEVELS OF VEHICLE AUTOMATION

LEVEL 0	No driving automation. The driver fully controls the car.
LEVEL 1	Driver assistance. The car can control either the speed or the steering, but not both at once.
LEVEL 2	Partial driving automation. The car can control both the speed and the steering at once, but a human driver must remain alert.
LEVEL 3	Conditional driving automation. The car can make driving decisions on its own. A human driver may need to take over in certain situations.
LEVEL 4	High driving automation. The car can drive itself in most situations. A human driver does not need to remain alert.
LEVEL 5	Full driving automation. The car can drive itself, no matter the driving situation.

The company SAE International outlines the six levels of driving automation. In 2024, cars up to level 3 were available for purchase.

MACHINE LEARNING AND ROBOTICS

Machine learning plays a huge role in the field of robotics. Robots designed to look like humans will use machine learning and NLP. This will make interactions between people and robots more natural. These robots may one day be able to work side by side with humans.

Another important use of ML is natural language processing (NLP). NLP is the ability of a computer to work with human language. Computers are now able to recognize and produce both the written and spoken word. People can use NLP to write things for them faster than they could by themselves. Companies are creating customer-service programs that can help customers solve issues. For example, the programs can help customers answer questions about the company's product or service.

NLP is also being used to accurately translate text from one language into another. However, there are still things that NLP algorithms cannot do. For example, they cannot understand language in the same way that people can. In the future, researchers may improve NLP further.

Natural language processing is used to create chatbots, which are computer programs that can hold conversations with users.

Some people are concerned about the future of machine learning. They worry that ML could have bad effects. For example, some data is **biased**. ML algorithms trained on biased data may treat certain groups of people unfairly. In the future, people must take care to use ML technology responsibly.

GLOSSARY

autonomous (aw-TAH-nuh-muss) Something is autonomous if it is able to act without outside control. Autonomous vehicles are able to drive without the full control of a person.

biased (BYE-ust) Something is biased if it unfairly favors or disfavors someone or something. Machine learning algorithms trained on biased data may make biased decisions.

classifies (KLA-sih-fyze) A person or computer classifies something by placing it into a group of similar things. The k-nearest neighbors algorithm classifies data points into groups.

data (DAY-tuh) Data is information collected for a purpose. Machine learning algorithms are trained using data.

impulses (IM-pull-sez) Impulses are brief transfers of electrical energy. Brain cells communicate with each other using impulses.

processes (PRAH-seh-siz) Something processes something else if it performs a series of actions on it that lead to a result. A machine learning algorithm processes data to learn from it.

reinforcement (ree-in-FORSS-mint) Reinforcement is the act of encouraging a behavior. One kind of machine learning is called reinforcement learning.

sensors (SEN-surz) Sensors are devices that detect information from the real world, such as light or heat. Machine learning algorithms can learn from data gathered by sensors.

FAST FACTS

- Artificial intelligence is the ability of computers to solve problems that normally require human intelligence.
- Machine learning involves making machines learn in a way that resembles how people learn.
- Algorithms are step-by-step instructions for computers. Machine learning involves algorithms and a large amount of data.
- In the 1950s, Arthur Samuel wrote one of the first computer programs capable of machine learning. The program helped a computer learn how to play the game checkers.
- Computer vision and natural language processing (NLP) are two major areas of study for machine learning researchers.
- Some people worry that machine learning could have bad effects on the world. People must use machine learning responsibly.

ONE STRIDE FURTHER

- How could machine learning benefit society?
- What are some of the positives and negatives of vehicle automation? Would you be comfortable riding in a vehicle that is fully autonomous? Why or why not?
- What effects could poor-quality training data have on a machine learning algorithm?

FIND OUT MORE

IN THE LIBRARY

Kulz, George Anthony. *What Is Artificial Intelligence?* Parker, CO: The Child's World, 2025.

Robots and AI. New York: DK Children, 2023.

Schwartz, Heather E. *Medical Artificial Intelligence Breakthroughs.* Rochester, MN: Mayo Clinic Press Kids, 2024.

ON THE WEB

Visit our website for links about machine learning:
childsworld.com/links

Note to Parents, Caregivers, Teachers, and Librarians: We routinely verify our web links to make sure they are safe and active sites. So encourage your readers to check them out!

INDEX